A Fist Full of Poems

Poems for the Soul

FAITH

PEACE

HOPE

By

John Campbell Lemon

Published by
Heritage Publishing.US
Bradenton, FL

DEDICATION

To my wife Nancy, who listened patiently
and carefully to every word of every poem
in this book.
Such ears are precious.

THE POEM'S ARE COMING!

The poems are coming,

are coming and coming.

Some have already arrived.

Hooray!!

Poems delicious and sweet.

Poems dark and hard.

Poems inscrutable and difficult to read.

They just keep coming and coming.

What joy there is in writing.

The poems line up in mind.

They wait their turns patiently.

The line is very long

the poems strain for release,

they want to be free to be read.

And the poet leans back to reflect

on the miracle that is

the Word.

THE COURTROOM

"All rise", the command rings out,
that familiar bailiff's cry.
And the judge emerges, full of wisdom and power.
Before him sit the plaintiff and accused,
well defended.
The judge demands the case begin,
And only from the beginning.
And so, it starts.
Accusations, denials, who did what and when.
The story moves on and on.
Witnesses, rebuttals, and stories,
and victims too.
Actions thought forgotten are brought forth
before the judge.
There is no jury. This is a bench trial.
The judge has the final say.
And all the accused are found guilty.
The uproar is deafening, with outrage bursting forth.
The condemned meet their fate.
A fate so well deserved.
But a small group cheers with tears of joy.
These admitted to their crimes.

And He gives His Son's life to death.
A death for many guilty lives.
This hardly seems fair at all.
But then the Son rises from death.
This is the grand finale.
Wisdom and power triumphant.
The guilty gone and rescued safe.
And perfect justice done.

CONDEMNED

All humans stand condemned.
We all are condemned to death.
There is no escape,
no way out.
Death is the fate of all.
We all say "yes, but no, but no, no, no!"
No, we all cry in anguish,
the anguish of our hearts.
No, no to the certainty of death.
Do our heart cries change our fates?
Are we not condemned
because we say so?
And why death?
Death is the irrevocable loss of life.
We, mankind didn't make this
judgement, this condemnation
to death.
Yet here it is against all of us
and this has always been.
Was there ever a time,
say one-hundred million
years ago, when
mankind lived without the
shadow of death
following the days of his life?

4

No is the simple answer.
If this were a fact these people
would still be walking the earth.
Alongside us.
They are not.
Is this a problem? Not really.
There is a truthful answer.
An answer so clear and simple
that only a fool would
reject it.
And fools there are,
by the millions and billions.
And the answer Himself,
is God Almighty, the
Creator of heaven and earth
and all else that there is.
Why not accept this answer
and believe it as Truth?
There really is no alternative
that works as well as
this one does.

A FORTUNE RIDES

A fortune rides upon
the thoughts of human beings.
A fortune dreamed.
A fortune beyond measure.
A fortune out of reach,
a dream is all it is.
A dream and wish,
"oh, could it be?"
A cry heard over and over.
A fortune rides upon a
dream. And nothing more.
So empty, hollow, and depressing.
Can any fortune be claimed,
by dreams and wishes?
Only wealth and fame and power
in this world.
These empty, hollow, and depressing things.
These come and go and come again.
Only to go once more.
These things are water in a sieve.
Oh, empty dreams and thoughts!
Is there really nothing else?
Nothing else in another form?
Why yes, of course!

Another fortune rides.
This fortune is in the form
of God both visible and
invisible.
This pairing is found in
Jesus the God-Man.
Jesus is the fortune.
The fortune rides in Him.
Full and rich, uplifting and good.
Jesus is the fortune
of all eternity.

FIRE AND HAMMER

Fire burns and hammers hit.
Both can lead to destruction.
God says His own word is fire and hammer.
Formidable to say the least!
All this contained in the Book.
Take heed dear reader of these
Words,
that you not be consumed by the
fire,
nor smashed to bits by the hammer.
Unbelief and destruction go hand
In hand.
Whose hand are you holding?
If His, if Jesus's, you are saved.
If not, you are doomed to fire and destruction.
Smashed to bits by your own disbelief.

(JEREMIAH 23:29) "Is My word like a fire? Says the Lord
and like a hammer that breaks the rock in pieces."

SIFTING FOR GOLD

The miner scoops his pan,
into the creek's rushing water.
He scoops up a sludge of rocks, pebbles, and sand.
It is a watery mess.
Nothing of value seen yet.
But the miner skillfully sifts this mess of mud
and gradually the gold appears.
The rocks and dirt and muck are all washed away.
Only the gold remains.
Pure gold, nothing unclean.
Gold, acceptable to the miner.
His search for his perfect gold
is a perfection everlasting.
The miner, of course, is God Almighty who
Sifts through the ages of sinners.
Most remain rocks and sludge,
but some, through faith and belief,
become the gold God seeks.

FOLLOW THE LEADER

Follow the leader, we're always told.
Just follow the leader, he knows
and knows the way.
Just follow the leader.
But does he know and know the way?
How can we tell and test?
Or should we even try.
The easy way is just to follow.
To where we don't know or how.
What does this leader really know?
And do we really care?
Or is it that he is the leader and
that is enough. Why question, just
follow the leader.
A puffed-up leader all false and fake
Can sure look shinny and bright,
without question.
Follow a leader into a hell
or follow a leader to a heaven.
Which will it be?
Either hope for the best and take the chance
Or diligently dig out the truth.
And truth once found is pure gold
to the finder.

It takes some work and questions why
But the payoff is worth the effort.
Consider a heaven or a hell.
What do these words really mean?
Find out! Find out!
Your eternal future is in the answers that
you dig-out.
Follow sin into hell, the devil as your leader,
or follow good to heaven, God Almighty
as your leader.
A little work, a little digging and truth
Is laid bare.
Then the choice is easy.

HOPES AND DREAMS

Hopes and dreams,
we all have them.
Dreams come true; the stories tell us.
But often life
delivers
devastating blows.
Hopes crushed and dreams smashed.
Hearts broken; tears shed.
Anger and bitterness
often follow.
What to do?
Anger and bitterness
destructive for sure.
Is this what we want?
Is there a path
that leads away from these?
Yes, there is! The path
has a name,
Jesus the Christ.
He is the way and the life.
And He is a choice.
He is a dream fulfilled.
No tears nor broken hearts
with anger and bitterness banished forever.
Jesus is the way of joy and peace.

SAY IT AS IF YOU MEAN IT!

It is in your heart, correct?
A thought and feeling
You cannot dispel.
Nor do you want to, either.
So important, you cannot stand the pressure of it.
It must be said.
You really mean it!
Important above all else, And others must know, too.
Say it as if you mean it!
Say it out loud, loud, that is the way.
Let the peoples hear.
This is the message of life, Not just this life we live now.
But also, a life after this now life.
A precious life beyond.
You ask, "beyond"? Yes, beyond this now life.
Say as if you mean it!
What is it that you mean?
The Name to say is Jesus!
Born to earth and lived to die, to rise to second life.
So, can you, if you so choose? Just follow Him.
Say it as if you mean it! And if you do.
Your reward awaits you from above.

IN AND OUT

A jug holding milk is only
a container.
The container holds within that which must come out.
It is the contained that really matters, that really
counts, that has the real value.
The container is useful and important but only
for its purpose.
And out?
This is the outpour of that of value found within the
container.
When out, that which was contained, can perform
Its valued functions.
Could it be we humans are containers?
Jugs full of something?
Perhaps.
If so, then think. What is the most basic
comparison?
Good and evil, good for you!
So, we human beings are containers
Holding both good and/or evil.
Is there a way to tell what the container holds?
Of course there is. It is found in the outpouring.
Evil has its peculiar stench and bitter taste.
Good has its wonderful, sweet aroma and taste.
In and out.

14

NO EXCUSE

You do something bad.
How do you excuse yourself?
With excuses, of course.
We all love excuses.
A good excuse takes off the guilt.
Guilt.
No one likes guilt, being responsible.
Responsible means being guilty,
guilty.
Do you have an excuse?
An excuse for your guilt.
But there is no excuse.
Excuse means nothing.
Nothing is anything not from God.
Only God can produce an excuse.
This excuse has a name which is Jesus.
Jesus! Think about this name.
This is the name of the God/Man.
He offers an excuse. This excuse is His blood
shed on the cross.
Your excuse is Jesus,
The One and Only God.

IT'S COLD OUTSIDE

Shiver and judder,
the cold bites deep and sharp.
Who chooses such misery?
Its cold outside and dark.
But inside is bright and warm,
toasty even, by the hearth.
Who wouldn't want to be here,
Inside where it is bright and warm?
Who indeed.
An easy choice as all can see.
Warm is better than cold.
Yet, what if there were one condition?
A condition to permit inside?
A grievous condition.
A condition that demands evil.
Evil in all its forms.
Lies, hatred, rapes, and murders, thefts, and cheating,
Tricks and bribes, and swindles
Everywhere.
All warm and toasty. Committing their heinous
acts in comfort.
And you?

16

Your choice is to say yes to the warmth with
Its condition of evils.
Or no.
No means to be rejected and tormented
By those hoards in the warmth.
No also means not to the evils.
This is good and very good.
As good as evil is bad.
To stand against evil is to stand tall.
And be observed by a Power.
He has a reward for those who
Choose cold.
A reward called Heaven.
A place of great warmth and love
and no evil in sight.
This is the place where God Almighty dwells
And so will you.

THE FOG

Fog so thick it feels like soup,
thick and creamy.
It stings the skin and burns
the eyes.
Fog.
We live our lives in fog.
In thick soupy uncertainty.
What is next? What will happen?
Will things be alright?
We all wonder.
Fog.
The future is the fog.
No one knows the future, no matter how hard one tries.
One's efforts will aways be lies.
The foggy future always defeats
the very best efforts of men.
And yet.
The most important future of all,
can be known.
But how? And what is this most important
future?
Is it obvious?
Yes.

Where will we go when we die?

Heaven or hell

are the obvious choices.

We all wonder at least a little.

But how can we know for certain?

There is a book that tells us, it is called the Bible.

This book explains this clearly.

Believe the man Jesus

Is also God.

And his claims to be Savior to be true.

He is the open door

to heaven.

A future, fog free, secure, and eternally true.

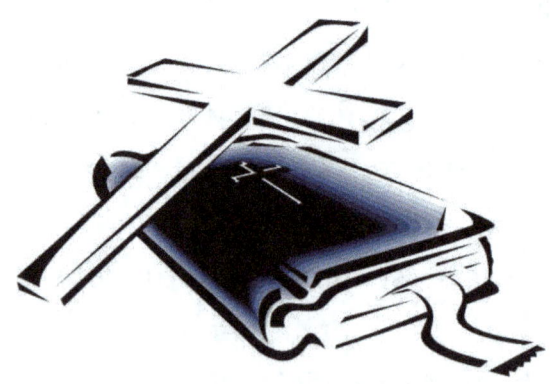

A SEAT

Do you have a seat?

A seat in the rocket ship to heaven.

If not, what do you think?

Well, to start, is there a heaven?

So, now we are intellectual.

Our thoughts tell us what?

There is no rocket ship, nor a heaven either.

Are you sure?

Sure.

What is sure?

Sure is certainty. But what is certainty?

And there you have it. Back to the start.

Do you have a seat?

The rocket ship is Jesus.

Do you have a seat in Jesus?

Jesus is also in heaven, and heaven is where God lives.

Do you have your seat?

Are you worried if you have no seat?

No seat, no rocket ship ride to heaven, no life with God.

Do you want heaven?

The opposite is hell.

You choose!

ALL OR NOTHING

Do you believe in God, do you believe God?
Why did Pharoah reject Moses and Aaron?
It's all or nothing really.
Either God exists or He doesn't.
Simple really, do you agree?
Perhaps you don't, then what?
Does your opinion matter, really?
No, even not at all.
Nor does mine.
Nor did Pharoah's. But Pharoah did choose to disbelieve.
And lots of bad things happened.
Real? Historical? Or just stories in a book.
A book of stories and fairy tales.
Flim flam at best and lies at worst.
But wait, who are the liars or liar?
Big question, yes.
It comes down to this:
If God is real, the stories are true.
If God is not real, the stories are false.
All or nothing. All or nothing.
Which way you go today?

I WANT

I want this for you.
What is this I want for you?
It is the path to heaven.
Heaven?
Yes.
What are you talking about?
Well, Jesus is God and Man in one person.
What!
This sounds weird.
So what.
Weird is not bad if it is good.
I want you to know Jesus.
Jesus is the human God.
What! Aren't all gods above man?
That is what people think.
They are wrong.
Jesus is God and Man.
Deny this truth and die, not just once but twice.
Once is bad enough.
But twice is twice as bad.
Do you like bad?
Then go for it!
Reject the God/Man Jesus.
The place you go
is grisly hell.

OFFER

An offer is proffered.
A good offer,
one would be wise to take it.
"Why wise, I don't even want what is offered."
That is the rub, isn't it?
You don't know what the offer is.
Therefore, you don't want it.
Well, this offer was made from the cross.
The cross from which Jesus hung and died.
The offer?
Entrance into His Kingdom.
Jesus, in case you didn't know,
is the King of Kings.
And kingdoms are ruled by kings.
There is much good to be gained
as a member of Jesus' Kingdom.
Heaven is a big one. Ever think of heaven?
Do you think you are going there
or do you just not care.
One sure thing is this.
Without belief in Jesus and accepting His offer,
you never will ever get there!

A CRIME

When a crime is committed
does punishment follow?
Is punishment automatic?
Is justice to be trusted?
Are judges to be trusted?
Is justice in freefall?
Unpunished crime
compares with on
requited love.
An empty pain, unfulfilled desires,
a longing for things to be right.
To be right!
Right! Righteous!
Punished crime is righteous.
One act deserves and is followed
by the other.
Yet, in much, if not most of history
And human life,
crimes go unpunished and
righteousness is punished.
This is human control at its lowest.
And low the humans go.
Low is their habitat, a desert, a swamp,
a thicket, a raging torrent.

A flood of no good.

A crime.

Will mankind judge himself?

Will the corrupt judge expose the bribe?

Will he give himself to justice?

Therefore, mankind needs help.

This help it resolutely rejects.

Ther are crimes, so many and so difficult
to count.

But there is One Man who also is God
who can easily tally the sum.

This sum convicts all men who live, have lived,
and will live. All mankind in total.

Crime demands punishment.

An eye for an eye.

Brutal crimes beg brutal justice.

But mercy?

Mercy is found in but one place.

The Head upon sits the crown.

The Prince of peace, the King of Kings.

A humble knee bent to Him brings mercy and joy forever.

A MAN'S PLANS

Plans are very important.
Who can do without them?
A plan is forethought,
a thing thought through.
A plan allows a building to be built.
One who wants to go
from here to there, needs a plan.
A plan helps to avoid failure,
A building collapse or a lost traveler.
But a plan is not a guarantee.
It only points the way.
A way in the darkness of future and time.
The past is illuminated by the light
of having happened.
This is not true of the future.
The lights come on in the present,
the present the forms the past.
The future is an unrealized hope.
"I will go there" only means "I intend to
Go there."
Who knows what may intervene?
We humans certainly don't!
Our lives are guesses and suppositions.
No matter how proudly we declare.

So, are we anxious about the future?
Well, yes and no.
We plan for this and fear that.
A schism so, so wide.
How can we live with yes and no active at the same time?
We do it because we must.
We have no alternatives.
But there is a book named bible
with many stories therein.
And many times, a people cry out
to a God who knows all things.
And He answers them who ask.
The future is known to Him.
The light of past things is cast forward
Into time unknown-
Unknown to us, humankind.
But not to the God who knows all things.

ON BENDED KNEE

On bended knee, face to the ground.
The bleak look of defeat its covering.
Bowing down to the one who conquered.
The one who conquered you.
Your fate hangs in the balance, life or
death.
Yet life in defeat is not life.
Not a pretty picture but common enough through
all of history.
To the victors go the spoils, hurrah!
But the spoils are you and your stuff.
On bended knee one honors the victor.
In pain, and fear, and dread.
Yet can bended knee be seen
In another light altogether?
Yes, another light altogether.
That light would be Jesus the Savior of the World.
On bended knee one honors Him, the Victor overall.
Instead of fear and dread, one on his knee
feels hope and joy.
Freedom for eternity
on bended knee
To Jesus.

REJECT

What did it take for you to
reject,
the One who claims to be God?
a claim like that is impressive.
But not enough for you.
You chose to reject God's claims.
What used you to make this choice?
Facts, perhaps.
Facts that you can prove.
Facts are facts only if they are true.
How do you know?
Go ahead and prove the fact that God
does not exist.
The fact is you will be the first person to prove
that God is a fake.
A lofty place indeed.
Oh, if you cannot prove God a fake,
what then?
You are really stuck,
in the quicksand of
what if.

RUNNING

To where does one run?
From what does one run?
Running.
We all are running.
Running to and running from.
Often running is to something good.
Often running is from something bad.
But, always running.
When does fatigue set in?
Fatigue must set in.
We all get tired,
sooner or later, often just sooner.
Is this all there is to life?
Just running to and from.
Do we ever get anywhere?
And what is where anyway?
If we run to something and get there,
can we lose it shortly after?
And if we run away from something,
can it overtake us, can we run away again?
can it overtake us, can we run away again?
Running, its all we really ever do.
Consider this, the following:

there is a run, that when
reached is fail safe.
Run to Jesus.
Reaching Jesus is reaching safety.
This safety is permanent
and eternal.
No more running to
or running from.

AVOID!

Evil thoughts, adulteries, fornications,
murder, thefts, covetousness,
wickedness, deceit, lewdness,
an evil eye, blasphemy, pride,
and foolishness.
Avoid these.
Avoid them'
These words have meaning,
they are not vague.

OBEY?

Is to obey a rope around a man's neck?
Does to obey mean be controlled?
If so, is this food or bad?
What think you the purpose be
of obey?
Does to obey result in
A servile role, inferior, even
threatened.
These latter are to be feared.
Under the thumb of another can be
a terrible place to be.
All this points to that which is to be obeyed.
This is the nerve of the matter.
An evil will produces evil results.
Those under suffer greatly.
A good will, though, is another and much better.
Obey and be blessed, that's the way.
Goodness follows blessing.
The results of this obedience hold peace,
gain, and joy, and much more.
So, when confronted with choice to obey,
if it is God, always say yes.

BELIEVE

Mankind's history shows
one try after another.
And failure is common and rampant.
Man's best-efforts crumble and fall.
Is there anything left?
Remember that belief is choice.
What choices then are offered.
Pick and choose and rummage through
the great pile of options.
Tired yet worn out too.
Such a task, and so driven too.
But one choice does shine through.
and rises to the top.
This choice is a glowing book
a one of a kind in millions.
This book named the BIBLE
was written by God and

CREDIBLE

That which is believable is credible.
Credible, believable, some sort
of truth.
Oh, one hopes it is truth.
Yet, we all know lies are believable,
as are deceptions.
Then what is credible? What is believable?
Is effort required to test for truth?
Is something credible just because it is out there?
Maybe.
But does truth always offer profit and gain?
The merchant who tells customer his products
Are inferior is a truthful man,
where is his profit though?
So, layers exist and hoops to jump through,
some hoops ever with fire!
Is it good to lie to cheat another,
for profit?
For public glory we lie again and say,
"cheating is bad."
We all want what is best for us.
What is best for us in our own eyes.
Someone else is watching though.
He is recording every lie and more.

No one is immune from His gaze.

All are seen as if naked.

All will be brought into court

All are guilty of lie after lie

And often ever so much worse.

In court there is The Judge.

The Someone who was watching.

No clever lie can fool this One.

And the guilty are judged for punishment.

All lie, all guilty, all judged, all to be punished.

This is indeed a grim fact.

No wiggle room, no mercy at this stage.

Wait though, is there another stage?

Yes, the credible stage, the stage of each
man's life on earth.

Those who find God's claims credible
and believe the Truth expressed,
are offered mercy, they believe.

Their lies and crimes are forgiven, but not
without a cost.

Their crimes beg punishment as fulfillment of
the cycle.

For that the God/Man Jesus came to earth
in mortal flesh.

His death paid the horrid price for the believer's
mercy given.

AN OPEN DOOR

An open door!
Sounds inviting, an invitation in,
in to go inside.
But wait a bit.
Let's think a minute.
Is a happy crowd
or a vicious mob,
waiting on the other side?
Do we know which it is?
Of course we don't.
How could we?
We do not know the future, how can we?
Isn't the future just a guess?
But a door is before us.
We do know this.
How do we know?
We just do and always have.
The big clue is death. Death in the door.
And we all die.
This is the door we all face!
An always present door.
We will all enter and pass through.
And to what and where, if anywhere,
will we go?

Do you care?

If not, you are a gambler.

Just a roll of the dice, a spin of the wheel.

The outcome is up to chance!

Chance, happenstance, a could be, a maybe...?

Feeling lucky?

But what if luck is not involved.

What if there is Truth, eternal Truth beyond the door of death.

What about that?

The door will always open, thus the open door.

The door that opens onto

a happy or vicious crowd.

You choose the crowd you want

or leave this choice to chance.

Chance gets you the vicious crowd.

The happy crowd has chosen Truth.

This Truth is Jesus Christ.

Love and joy and peace are theirs

and yours forever too.

But you must choose Jesus.

THE BET

Would you bet your life?
Would you put your very existence
On the line?
This is the bet all men face,
just by being alive.
You bet your life!
Yet, on what?
The future is never clear,
though plans and promises
fool the unwary.
So, what is the bet?
And can it be won or lost?
The bet.
Your life is on the line.
And you must choose
and it is either or.
Your bet is placed at the
cross of Christ.
And your death reveals
your choice.
No do overs, either or.
A bet on Christ is the winner

A LITTLE CHILD

What does a little child know?
Not too much really.
Certainly not as much as an adult.
Adults are grown people.
They have learned much.
They often think they know
enough to be masters
of their fates.
Not true, of course, and yet, an
impediment of great power.
What a man know may block him
from learning what he needs
to know.
Thus, the childlike mind
is the mind preferred.
Preferred for what?
To learn the precious knowledge
offered by the Son of God.
His Name is Jesus the Christ.
Man's knowledge is a cloud,
a vision blocker.
The cloudless view of a child's mind
allows a man to see.
Stop staring at your feet mere man.
Look up and see God.

BECOME COMPLETE

Complete.
Ok, all the pieces came with the puzzle,
all the parts for the job.
You get the idea, everything is there,
complete.
How does this work in a human life?
Is a person complete?
A checklist of parts of the physical body
tells the tale.
A missing organ or limb or two
crafts the count.
But what of the inner man,
the spirit man of the spirit of life?
This is the person we meet, the person we are.
Without the spirit of life, the body is just
Flesh and bones, inanimate.
Care to find out what a dead man thinks?
What then can be considered complete
in the living man, alive by the spirit of life?
"Become complete. Be of good comfort, be of one mind,
live in peace, and the love of the God
of and peace will be with you.

Can one say, in truth, that he
has these things,

without the spirit of God?
Ignore God at your peril.
Any other comfort and peace
is a mirage.
The fooled will discover their folly,
in due time, at the end.
Then it will be too late,
now is the time to act.
Say, "yes, Jesus my Savior"!

CAN YOU BELIEVE THIS?

An all-powerful spirit
says to Himself and the others too,
let's make some things.
Ok, they say.
We'll make a universe.
How about that!
This universe will be huge
because there is plenty of room.
There is nothing there yet,
you see.
This all-powerful Spirit also
decides
to create some living creatures too.
Not just rocks and air and water.
And so, this Spirit, all three together
agreeing,
speaks the words that bring the worlds alive.
Can you believe this?
Can you prove that this is not so?
The question "can you believe this" is
A matter of life and death.
As this Spirit known as God has
also said,
believe and live
or deny belief and die.

This is a good offer, really,
and the only one that works.
Roll the dice and deny
And end up the loser.
Just believe the obvious.

MANY WAYS

A massive danger
lies ahead.
A danger unthinkable.
Yet, how to escape?
Is there a way to escape?
Are there ways to escape?
With no escape
a certain fate awaits.
A fate severe, a fate
so ghastly,
all should deeply fear.
Yet, many snooze, so
unaware.
Their doom is set in stone.
Only the alert can escape.
But what way or ways
exist?
Many ways do lay before us.
Though only one brings freedom.
Choose wrong and never get away
from the danger so ghastly
it is unspoken.
The one Way involves a Power
far greater than the danger.

45

This Power is in plain sight for
all who's vision's clear. This
Power reveals Himself
In everything and everywhere.
He even wrote a book about Himself.
A book the wise will always read.
Many ways are of no help
Only the One will do.
Choose the Way explained in the book
and escape the
ghastly danger.

WHO ARE THE CHILDREN?

Who are the children?
Silly question is this.
The children are the little ones
and the young as well.
Right?
The man of ninety-five years
is still the child of his parents,
parents long gone,
though still alive in him.
The point of this is this,
we are all children
now and forever more.
There is no escaping the egg and seed.
But that is physical and death
claims us all.
Can we humans be children
of other parents?
Of Satan or God?
Think and think hard
on this thought.
and add eternity.
Our bodies die, but do we?
Have we souls that never die?
If so, then think and think hard.
Whose child do I want to be?

UNFORGIVABLE

Do you want to go to hell?
Really want to go.
A sure thing/
Unstoppable.
Perfect 100% odds of success.
Just say no. Just say no.
Really simple, really.
Some would call it a no brainer.
And a no brainer it is.
For sure and for certain.
But why go to hell when
you can just as easily
choose heaven?
That is not a no brainer.
That choice needs thought.
Thought that asks "what is better for me"?
Heaven is better by far.
Heaven is happy while hell is horrible.
Sunny days or hurricanes.
God, the Creator, offers both.
The ones who love Him get heaven
and the ones who hate Him get hell.

NOTHING

Can you imagine nothing.
Not a single thing.
No earth, not sun and moon, nor stars.
Not even a speck of dust.
No atoms nor protons either.
Just nothing.
Does your head ache yet?
We simply cannot do it.
We are all something
living in something
with something all around us.
But it wasn't always this way.
Before the beginning there really was nothing,
just as described above.
Only a spirit existed, no matter at all to be found.
And then the beginning came.
A power and force so great
as to bring the universe into being.
Plants, and suns, and stars.
As well as living things too.
You, a living thing, reading these
words right now,
are a created being.
And very special too!

You are made in the image of God.
This God, this heavenly Spirit,
Is the source of all things.
From nothing He made everything,
everything including you.
This God is named Jesus.
He lived on this earth too.
He gives us everything,
if only we would ask.
And if we ask, believing Him,
He will even give us
Heaven.

OUT OF ORDER

"You are out of order!"
We all know what this means.
Someone has broken a rule or rules.
Is this a bad thing?
What a mammoth question!
Groups, families, communities, states, and cultures and
religions,
are all built on rules.
Rules rule.
Yet, as the phrase goes, "rules are made to be broken."
Is this true? How much thought
put we into this question?
Too much and not enough to make a good answer.
"You are out of order!" A rebuke of force and purpose.
The meaning is that you have broken rules, you are
caught and now must stop.
So far so good.
Rules at their best bring order not chaos.
As a steady thing order is superior to chaos.
A government of and by bad rules begs a payment of chaos.
Chaos is a curse.
This is a recycling pattern.
Then, to what or to whom shall we turn for
consistent order and rules?

51

There is One. Please research all the others.
It is important note that this One claims to be Order itself.
A big claim, the biggest! But is it true?
Is the claim to be Order true?
Another mammoth question.
How do we, as liars, deceivers, cheaters,
and brutes, test for Order and Truth?
We do not, we cannot, we are unable.
We sink under the weight of our lies.
We must let Order test Truth.
The testimony of an honest man is truth.
The One is an honest man. The One and
Only.
Jesus proves Himself, Order and Truth never fail, Order and
Truth
are always visible and in plain sight.
We who are weighted down choose to be blind.
We choose chaos as our king and
deny the True King of Order and Truth.
His rules bring peace through

PERMISSIVE POWER

There is always someone bigger,
Smarter, faster and on and on.
So where do you and I fit?
Maybe a little power, perhaps a lot,
oh, and maybe nearly none at all.
But always someone with more power.
Go up the chain of hierarchy,
go as far as you can go.
Names, positions, places, possessions
this climb makes one dizzy and faint.
And the powerful?
Do they all realize they are not at the top?
Who then is the top above whom
there is no other?
Take a guess. Ok, take another.
The answer is the deity.
The God, the All Powerful
God Almighty,
the chief resident of the universe.
And He dispenses power
permissive power that only
the wise perceive.
In fact, this God Almighty
distains the proud and vain.

He prefers the humble.

The humble know in whom and where
real power resides.
So, if you think you are
flying high on your own wings
of power,
prepare for a crash and disaster.
His Power won't lift
your proud wings.

COMPLICATED

How complicated does human
life have to be
to push God out the door.
Tech and gadgets, stories, and games,
diversions of all and many
sorts.
Many with merit is a small
context.
But none even close to God's equal.
Why be last when you can be
second?
Acknowledge that there is only
One.
The One God Almighty, a few are second and most are
last.
Lost in human's complexity.

SALVATION IS NOT...

Salvation is not a reward.

Certainly not as one thinks.

Mankind likes to climb ladders

to see who reaches the highest.

Climbing the ladder of success, that is the dream and goal.

Murders and wars, deaths, and destructions

occur on this upward ladder.

Some bright spots too, to be sure.

The world is not all evil.

Or is it?

Consider the bright spots.

Spots of light dotting the field of dark.

So, what about salvation?

This vehicle to ride up to heaven.

Can a man climb a ladder

and, in victory, claim his reward?

If this were true, then most humans

would dump the dark for sure.

But wait, what?

No, salvation is not a reward.

"What is it then," men cry out

in voices of desperation.

Not a reward? How can we

earn our way into heaven with God?

56

Where is our control?
Your answer, you never had any control.

Oh, you can buy and sell, and do the stuff of life,
but never, ever control your goal of heaven.
Heaven is a gift.
And the giver is God Almighty who calls Himself "I Am."
He identifies Himself in His Book,
clearly and uniquely.
He offers the gift.
The gift has a name too, JESUS THE CHRIST.
Yes, the One who died on a wooden cross.
Only he can let you into heaven.
In this you do have control.
The control to believe or not. This is up to you.
Jesus inspects people's hearts
For the truth in their belief.
Real believers move to heaven,
The others stay on the ladder.

COMPETING WITH GOD

Pick your fights, right.
Pick the ones you think you will win.
To pick a fight you surely will lose
is a fool's choice.
So many fools. So many.
Some say there is no God.
Some choose other gods.
Some just don't care at all.
But there it is in everyone's
life.
The knowledge of God Almighty.
This God Almighty does not need
to fight,
He has already won.
He created the universe and all that is in it.
He has nothing to prove.
So, fools decide to compete.
They have already lost,
so, what is the point?
They have nothing that they can
prove.
Just huff and puff and wear
yourself out.
There is nothing to gain
by competing with God.

SWARM

Take a stick,
a big, long stick.
And be ready to run.
Scope out your route, the way
you will run.
When you strike the hornet's nest.
A nest full of peaceful, though well-armed,
hornets.
Strick their hive though and look out.
all hell breaks loose at once.
How foolish one thinks of those
who pick up the stick and strike.
Strike the hornet's nest.
Do they know what will become?
A flurry of angry insects, armed to hurt,
kill, and destroy.
Strike their nest and pay the price,
How fast do you think you can run?
The hornets always get their prey,
Their simple foolish prey.
Just as Adam and Eve struck the nest
In the garden of Eden
The swarm has been on us.
Stinging, killing, hurting, and destroying.

DAILY TROUBLE

A day without trouble is rare
and when one occurs
it brings joy.
Yet, most people worry about tomorrow
a time we cannot control.
Tomorrow is the future
a dark and black hole that
no light of man can penetrate.
Only daydreams and plans can
come forth.
There is a light, however, that
can and does
penetrate the darkness.
It is the Light of the Son of God.
Jesus' light penetrates all.
Things, people, and time.
And there is never trouble
in Jesus's days.
He to us from heaven
not to worry about
tomorrow.
Focus instead on the of
troubles of this day.

And trust Jesus to help you through.
Choose the Gospel of the Kingdom of God
above all else in your world.
You will receive Jesus as your King.

And kings are full of power.

I AM JUST A COLLANDER

Every day I am filled.
Filled with all sorts of things.
Some good, some not so.
Some stay in me
some drain out.
I am just a colander.
But unlike a real
colander
I have a choice.
A choice of what stays in
And what flows out.
This choice is grand and powerful.
It can even be over life or death.
We are all colanders, really.
Good and bad always come in.
It is what goes out that matters.
Choice is always choice no matter what.
A colander sitting in a sink
mindlessly lets the fluids through.
We as people have a harder job to do.
Sometimes good seems bad
and the opposite too.
So how to tell them apart.
There is a standard.

This standard is found in
one book.
The one written by God Almighty.
Who better to know good
than the Author and Creator.
Be wise and learn
and turn from evil.
Be the colander
He designed you to be.

WHAT DOES IT TAKE?

What does it take to know I AM,
the name of Almighty God?
Does it take money? Then only the rich
could know Him.
Does it take fame? Then only the famous
could know Him.
Does it take power? Then only the powerful
could know Him.
Does it take beauty? Then only the beautiful
could know Him.
What does it take then?
Does God, "I AM," give us clues?
Why yes, of course He does.
It is all explained in His wonderful
Book.
You know it as the Bible.
Written by God, "I AM," and infused
with all divine power,
All anyone needs to know of
what it takes is there!
The only catch is in your heart.
Is it soft, and open, and willing?
If not, you will never know
What it takes.

A NEEDLE AND A CAMEL

What do a needle and a camel
have in common?
Nothing obvious to be sure and clear.
A camel is a very large
and ungainly beast.
A needle is a small piece of metal with a hole.
One is living the other is not.
But both have eyes and an eye.
Oh! There is the connection that
they share in common!
Now what?
Well, there is a story in an old book,
a book written by God.
This story tells of a camel trying to
get through the eye of a needle.
Ha! That's an absurd story.
And of course it is.
Just as absurd as a man
thinking his own way into heaven.
Jesus is the eye of the needle and allows all who believe
to pass through Him,
the eye of the needle, to enter glorious
Heaven.

JUST ASK

All you have to do is ask.

Just ask.

You know you want to.

So, why don't you?

Just ask.

He will give you what you need.

Just ask and He will give you what you want.

What is that

you need and want?

Do you know?

What! You don't know what you need and want?

Health and happiness,

new car, better job.

All things we hear we want,

food for our stomachs,

fine clothes on our backs,

money in the bank.

All good things within reason.

But they don't last.

And neither will you!

The day is coming when the door shuts on your life.

Where is your stuff then?

But what if there is something else
To hope for, to even
take with you through another door.
Would you be interested?
Are you interested?
Just ask, the door has a name, Jesus.
His name means He saves His people.
just ask Him this,
"will you accept me, a sinner"?
Just ask and the answer is
yes.

A ONE- WAY ROAD

Life itself is a one-way road.
And all its traffic
Flows one way.
For some it is a short
journey.
Others longer and
much tougher.
But for all travelers
the road comes
to its end.
For some the journey
is rough and hard.
For some the journey
is smooth and easy.
But all travel to the
destination.
This destination is death.
Death departs us from
the road.
In fact, death is a fork.
A few go this way,
but most go that.
It's all foretold you see.

No matter easy or hard
we all make a
commitment
during our journey.
A commitment for or against
One man.
An amazing Man, also God
who directs us travelers
the way of our choice.
We choose; we do. Do we want
to travel with Him
whose Name is Jesus?
The fork in the road is life or death.
Life is with Jesus,
death is without Him.
This death is a one-way road.
A road paved with pain and
regret.
This is all so easily avoided.
Just choose Jesus the first time.

ASHAMED

Jesus says if you are
ashamed of me,
I will be ashamed of you.
The one follows the other.
To choose to be ashamed of Jesus
is to choose to bring
His displeasure.

This would be the displeasure of God.

Is one's personal pride
so worth this
that God's displeasure
is sought.
Jesus, whose death on the cross
and subsequent
return to life,
is the God who decides
where all reside forever.
On that day when you stand
face to face with Jesus
and you hear,

"I am ashamed of you"
brace yourself for
eternity in hell
Gnashing of teeth and eternal regret
as well as fire and brimstone.

A MAN'S THOUGHT

How foolish it is
for a man to think
he can send himself to heaven.
What vehicle can he choose
to accomplish the impossible feat?
A rocket ship, a large balloon, a drug
or two or three.
What are his options?
There are none. Not a single one.
So, no trip to heaven then.
But the man knows he must die
and what happens then?
Nothing? Or something, or what?
It won't be heaven for sure.
Then what should this man think?
He still wants to go to heaven.
This compelling feeling is deep
within his soul.
And then he thinks
the most profound thought
Ever in his life,
"Jesus is the way".
He thinks, Jesus claim to be man and
God is true.
Heaven is through Him.
"This is certainly for me!"

END OF THE ROAD

The end of the road,
the journey complete.
There is no more path
to follow.
The road is a history.
A history of a life.
A life no longer lived.
As with a book
the last page of the last chapter
is written.
Those left behind mourn
this light of life
now extinguished.
Though this road of life has ended
the story of life has not.
A new road opens,
no two.
One is wide and terrifying,
the other narrow
and inviting.
The road taken the first time
determines
which of the two is next.

The first road travelled
with Jesus
will open to the inviting road next.
All others take the wide
and terrifying next road.
Fire and pain, remorse, and grief
await those without
Jesus.
Wisdom says that in the first life
the road with
Jesus is the way.

MAN, THE CHAMPION

Man, us, who we are. Mankind, people.
Humans, beings. Created from nothing or from existing slime?
Man, the champion. The hero is the victor,
the winner.
Who could want anything else?
Take home the trophy and put it out for show.
Victory, hero, and champion.
Sounds so very good!
Sounds to be just what we want.
To stand in front of the crowd, the cheering
crowd, to be the hero, and the champion.
Man.
But is man worthy?
What makes a champion worthy?
Just victory?
Just a championship?
This is the question of eternity.
Who really is worthy?
The man who leads his men to conquest?
Or is this just for a moment?
How long is a champion a champion?
What about the next match?
Champion after champion and on and on.
And on to forgetfulness.
Is man the champion, or even a champion?

What merits this anyway?
And so many men, so many champions,
so many victors and victories,
who cares!
Too much. What about just one champion?
Just one, we all can breathe a sigh of relief.
Just one but who?
Who could be the only champion?
Well, it would help if it were God Almighty!
This champion has a name which is Jesus.
Jesus the Christ-Messiah, the Son of God Almighty.
He is the One and Only Champion overall.
We do have a Champion and He is both God and Man,
amazing, yet worth believing.
The Champion, Jesus, is worthy of His Title.

NO SHEPHERD

What does it mean to have no shepherd?
What is shepherding anyway?
Isn't a shepherd one who cares for sheep?
Out in the fields.
Danger lurks out in the fields.
And sheep cannot fend for themselves.
Sheep epitomize the concept of prey.
Prey that is the predators dream.
Prey that is not alert, nor aware
of dangers all around.
Prey that passively chews its food
eyes impassively blank.
Prey have ears but do not hear
the sounds of danger all around.
Prey is living food, though not yet processed.
And, without a shepherd, the prey's
days are short lived.
Predators prowl and scheme
and even fight amongst themselves
for the easy prey before them.
No shepherd equals easy pickens
Are we humans, as sheep, defenseless easy prey?
We rarely think so. We think our own strength,

our brains, and wealth and things
will protect us from the dangers.
How wrong, so wrong are we in every way.
Our defenses are weaker than our foe's strengths.
Yet, we refuse to acknowledge this.
How wrong, so wrong are we in every way.
Our defenses are weaker than our foe's strengths.
Yet, we refuse to acknowledge this.
And so, we fall, as prey, to predators we
rarely see coming.
There is hope though, in this grim and dreary saga.
His Name is the Good Shepherd.
Perhaps you have heard of Him?
He has the rod and staff of a true shepherd.
The rod for the foes and the staff for the prey.
Would you like to know this, Shepherd?
His Name is JESUS. He is standing right in front
of you.
Recognize Him, want Him, believe, and believe in
Him.
And He will welcome you with open arms
And become your very own Shepherd.

PAY ATTENTION

Pay attention to what is written.

Pay attention to what is read aloud.

Pay attention to what you hear.

There is doom to pay if you don't!

Words are written that no one escapes.

Not even angels.

Words are read, those that are written,

that all must hear and weep.

These words that are written are power.

Not just powerful.

These words, when read, are power.

Not just powerful.

The power of all time and place is the author

of these words of Power.

And command.

The command is to read, to listen and obey.

And most don't.

Most don't pay attention; most don't read, most

don't listen.

This is to their disgrace and doom.

Pay attention then, to what is written and read.

See and hear and obey.

The belly of hell hungers for the food called

the inattentive.

A full belly will hell have.
Full of the witless and inattentive.
And hell bemoans the missed morsels
Of those who read and heard and obeyed.
The attentive, those who paid attention.

SALESMANSHIP

What kind of skill
does it take to sell
an undesired product?
Announce the product's many
flaws?
Extol the lack of virtues?
Emphasize the bitter
results from the use of the undesired product?
Of course not!
The skills needed would be salesmanship.
Lipstick on a pig, so to speak.
The goal is to make the undesired
as appealing as can be.
Make it so desirable
that only a fool would reject it.
Are you that fool?
Tricked, blinded, and fooled?
Fooled into believing hell is a
grand place,
by hiding what it really is.
Hell is death to light and all that is good.
The lipstick glosses over the ugly.
The salesman creates a mirage.
There is one defense.

His Name is Jesus.

He alone can dispel the mirage.

And those who claim Jesus,

claim life in the Light.

And escape the mirage of the

salesman.

SECURE YOUR FUTURE

The future is bleak, a dark place
of unknowns.
We people guess, of course, and have our hopes tool
But do we really know?
No, no to know!
How can mankind foretell the future?
It hasn't happened yet. It isn't history yet.
History we know. We can even rewrite it, though
rewriting is a lie.
Therefore, thoughts of securing the future
are all false, there is no way to do it.
Or is there?
There is one way, known to a few,
who know their futures are secure.
Who are these people, these geniuses
who can foretell the future?
How do they differ from you and me,
us to be in general?
To secure one's future only one thing
must be done.
No genius, wealth, privilege, or tricks
are needed.

Just this one thing...
Belief.
Belief in the One, the God Man
whose name is Jesus.
His name means, "Savior of His people."
Those who believe have a secure future,
an eternity of success and joy.
Those who don't believe?
Their future is secured in disaster.

WELCOME

Come on in you are welcome here.
Our doors are open to you.
No, you don't need to dress up,
You just come as you are.
You are welcome here.
You say you've done bad things.
bad things to block your
entry.
Hey, we've all done bad things,
none of us should be here.
Come on in you are welcome here.
When you do come in
you will find a pure and clean
place.
This place won't be dirtied by your
dirt.
This place will clean you up.
Come on in you are welcome.
This is a joy filled place.
You will need to leave where you are.
Where you are is an unhappy place.
Come on in you are welcome.
No, you don't need a ticket.

But you do need to do one thing first.
Say hello to the owner
who opens His home to you,
and acknowledge that He is
the Master.

WE ALL NEED WATER

All living things need water.
Even fish!
Animals, bugs, plants, and humans.
We all need water.
And without water we all die.
Remember that houseplant you forgot
to water? Dried dead and crunchy.
Is this an accident?
An accident that affects all living things
and always has
from the beginning for Millenia of years.
Hmmm? What kind of thinking
would be needed to
reject this obvious truth.
Why, the kind of thinking that most
humans have thought through the ages.
And this is to think we did it all.
Or just plain blind luck.
But certainly not a supernatural being
who knows everything, is everywhere
at once and is all powerful.
Why, that is ridiculous, right?

Add to this the fact that He, this supernatural
being, showed up on earth
as a man.
Laugh, laugh out loud.
But He is a threat to human
belief in luck.
So, kill Him why don't you. And you already did.
Done and done, but for this,
He came back to life in three days.
This supernatural being, who has a Name,
is Jesus the Christ, the Savior.
Oh, by the way,
water was His idea.

SAT DOWN TO EAT

A man sat down to eat.
No thanks came forth
from him.
His food unblessed, he ate it all.
No sense of grace or gratitude.
The food accomplished its
intended purpose.
It nourished the ungrateful
man's body.
The great plan was working
as it would.
Providing health and good.
And what of the ungrateful man?
His benefit was his.
His body fed and full.
But his spirit went
unfed and poor.
A weak and poor spirit leads to
spiritual starvation
and eventual death.
"Who cares!" you say. OK,
for now.

But death of body will come, always comes,
for everyone.
And then the dead spirit wakes up
to live in fear and terror.
Fear and terror for eternity.
The ungrateful man refused
to honor the source
of his life and his food.
And what is this Source?
God, the Almighty I AM, of course.
And Jesus His Son
showed us all the way
of gratefulness and trust.
To not follow Him to your peril,
and reap the reward of terror.

SNAKE ON A STICK

A snake, a serpent, can be
a scary thing.
Some are deadly but some are not.
They all slither around on their
bellies.
God used deadly snakes
to train His people Israel.
His people, as we are too, were rebellious.
A gentle, "stop it," wouldn't do.
Something more forceful was needed.
Welcome the serpent.
With discipline comes death.
Death to rebellion. A turn-around.
God turned His people around with
serpents and death.
Then He put a bronze serpent on
a stick.
And placed it high for all to see.
Look upon this serpent
and be healed.
So too today, we as a rebellious
people,
can look upon Jesus,

lifted up.
For all the world to see.
All one must do
to be healed is look upon
this Savior,
and believe
and be healed.

STRIVE

The world strives. Every day.
All mankind strives and always has.
Strain, struggle, and strive.
So much effort, energy, pain and purpose.
All to win a game, conquer a nation,
get a gold watch at retirement.
Then, who or what remembers,
the victories, gains, and goals.
All accomplishments too.
These all slide into the mists of time
recalled only on pages of history books.
Strive.
Why? The struggle is really only for
the moment.
Let it all out, the blood, sweat, and tears.
Enjoy the now.
Puff up in pride, bask in the glow,
revel in adulation.
It is all you get, just for now alone,
and then it slips away.
A building built; a building burnt.
Only smolder and ashes remain.
What was the point?

A question asked with full meaning.
Man's moments go up
only to fall back down again.
What is the point?
We live in the moment, the now.
We all must eat and all the rest.
As a canoe is paddled along a stream
We, mankind, strive.
Our moments behind us.
And the God burns it all up.
A clean, fresh start unfolds.

WHEN NONSENSE RULES

We all know nonsense
means what it says.
No sense!
So how does one make sense
of it,
of nonsense and all its meanings.
How many examples of nonsense can one
person produce?
A handful, five fingers and toes or
maybe score and scores?
Scores and scores and more and more
and even more and more.
Nonsense rules!
Leaders reign, yet nonsense rules.
Mankind strains for sense.
Elusive sense.
Evasive sense.
Yet is it true that sense eludes
And sense evades?
If true we humans are to be most pitied.
Our lives and futures doomed and damned
by the absence of what matters.

We live our lives in a swirl of nonsense,
of chaos, darkness and fear.
Gain is loss, love is hate, health
Is sickness, wealth is poverty.
Is there no way out?
Of course there is, cheer up!
It is, or rather, He is right in front of you.
You see Him every day and night and feel Him
with every breath you take.
He is right in front of you, beside you, above and
below you.
He is everywhere.
And He makes sense of it all.
He is the Creator, JESUS.
Yes, that Lamb to Lion One.
He longs to give you sense, the sense of understanding.
Yes, chaos and nonsense are everywhere,
but He JESUS is the answers.
Trust Him and believe He is the One,
and revel in the results.

WHAT WAS CAN NEVER BE AGAIN

The past. Back then. So good.

Wasn't it?

Was it?

Maybe not, maybe so.

Yet, nothing stays the same.

And there is no going back

to live in actual time.

So, we daydream and reminisce

and ponder times past.

But were people happier than they are now?

Struggles, battles, hatred, and crime,

are all part of life for all time.

Cain killed Able the bible says.

These men were the sons of Adam and Eve,

the first human parents.

Murder is the first crime recorded in print.

Is there a time in the past when things were

really good?

No.

No time that ever was good if good means no crime

and evil.

Oh, wait!

There was such a time and there will be again.
The time before was before the bite of apple Eve took.
And the one to come.
Read the bible to get your clues,
but they are right out in the open.
A place called heaven is the name.
A perfect place. No crime for hate
nor evil thing.
Such as these will all be gone.
Gone for good and goodness sake.

I can do ALL THINGS *through* Christ *who* STRENGTHENS *me.*
–Phillippians 4:13

UNBELIEF

What a marvel is unbelief.
The mind shuts as a gate.
Slams shut in some cases.
Unbelief is hard to believe
When the unbelief
is of the Truth.
A thing happens in full and
plain view,
a real and true thing.
Yet, some there are who would deny.
They deny in unbelief.
They reject the undeniable
replacing it with a lie.
These fabrications, so easily and
quickly made
are false and untrue
to their core.
But they are believed.
This happened to Jesus in His
hometown.
He was too familiar to them.
They couldn't believe that
this carpenter's son
could do what He did.

Is this you?
when you refuse
to believe.
Have you some false fabrication
you hold up as defense
against the Savior of
the World?
His goal is to be believed
and to share His saving
power.
You slam the gate in His face.

ULTIMATELY

Ultimately everything depends on
something.
Your guess is as good as mine.
Yet, true this is.
No air leads to death.
This theme repeats on and on.
This is obvious in the physical world.
Measuring, weighing, collecting data.
These all reveal the story.
But what of the immaterial, the spiritual,
the ephemeral?
How does one measure these?
Yet ultimately everything depends on something.
Upon what then does spirit depend?
It must depend on something.
Everything is connected to everything else,
in some way.
Ultimately an answer is there to be found.
And found at the beginning.
Beginning you ask?
Did what we now know as existence
always exist?
Probably not.

So, there had to be a beginning.
Ultimately the beginning depended
upon its start.
This start is explained in one word.
God.

Lord
I pray
to be *Led* to
and by you

TRY TO IMAGINE

TRY TO IMAGINE.
IMAGIN IF YOU WILL,
A WORLD WITHOUT STORMS, NO CYCLONES, HURRICANES,
AND SUCH.
OR FIRES THAT BURN WHOLE FORESTS
TO ASH.
AND PEOPLE AND HOMES AS WELL.
AND CITES AFIRE WITH DEATH AND DESTRUCTION,
AND WARS, CRIPPLING, AND MAIMING.
OH, AND LIES AND DECEPTIONS, GOVERNMENTS
RUN AMUK.
NO PLACE TO RUN, NO PLACE TO HIDE.
THE WHOLE EARTH IS SWARMED
AND SOAKED IN ROT, EVIL, AND HELL ON EARTH.
SPEAKING OF HELL,
DO YOU THINK MY DESCRIPTION THUS FAR
IS BAD?
SINCE ALL MUST DIE, WHAT THEN?
ONE AND DONE, OR SOMETHING ELSE?
THAT ELSE IS ON ALL MEN'S MINDS.
WHAT HAPPENS AFTER THES LIFE ENDS?
IS IT NOTHING OR SOME FORM OF LIVING?

WE MAKE OUR CHOICES SINCE WE
CANNOT REALLY KNOW.
OUR STORMS AND WARS WE KNOW
FOR SURE, BUT AFTER?
BUT WE ALSO KNOW MANKIND
PONDERS, AND ALWAYS HAS.
IS THERE A HEAVEN AND HELL?
NOT ONE OR THE OTHER BUT
BOTH AS TWINS
OF AN ETERNAL FUTURE
FOR EACH PERSON.
FOR EACH ONE IT IS ONE OR THE OTHER.
WHICH ONE IS BASED ON TWO THINGS.
AN ALL-POWERFUL GOD AND OUR OWN CHOICE.
CHOSE GOD WHOSE NAME IS JESUS
AND HEAVEN AWAITS YOU.

REJECT HIM AND HELL IS YOUR FATE.

TRY TO IMAGINE.

TRAVEL PLANS

Travel plans,
well thought through, bringing the journey to life.
One plans ahead, where to go,
what to do and see.
And where to stay and even what to eat.
All laid out on the kitchen table.
A feast of the future,
on which we can nibble and chew.
These tasty plans are our treats
For the coming days and weeks.
The anticipation grows with each bite.
And, sure enough, the day of departure
arrives.
And off we go!
Our destiny so carefully planned out.
But what if, instead,
We simply booked a flight.
We tell the agent "you pick where and when we go."
A different trip for sure!
Excitement yes, but also fear,
our destination so unknown.
Not much fun in the pondering,
there is nothing to ponder.

This is how it is with most of us,
when we consider heaven.
A great place to go,
but what's really there, and will we
really like it.
And do we really believe it,
anyway?
Belief is the ticket,
belief in Jesus the Christ.
No travel to heaven
without this golden ticket.
No golden ticket leads to
a trip,
to a very unpleasant place.
So, why don't the holders
of golden tickets
care more about their trips.

THE GRAVE

What do we think when we think of the grave?
Death, of course, death for sure.
One must be dead
to deserve the grave.
Is the grave the inheritance of man?
Is the grave the goal after all?
And what of hope?
Is our hope only in the grave?
And death?
Thoroughly certain.
There is no way out of this certain future.
All humans die.
Quite grim really, don't you say?
As grim and hopeless as anything.
All goals and successes of a man
are stamped "so what."
GRIM, GRIM, GRIM.
No hope at all, what is the point of anything?
What is the point of striving in life?
Why not just trudge and slog along through one's life?
Nothing follows us into the grave.
Only our remains remain.
And yet, what of the talk of heaven?

A wonderful place to be!
The grave is only a portal
for passage to this place.
Do we need to pass a test?
there are neither tickets nor passports
as we in life perceive.
But there is one simple test.
Do you believe God exists,
in three-part form for sure.
Try this on for size then.
The God named Jesus, one of the three,
lived on earth as one of us.
And we killed Him.
But He did not stay dead.
Instead, He rose to life again,
His hands outstretched to us.
Instead of wrath and vengeance,
He offers love and heaven.
Refuse this if you will,
but heaven has a twin.
A bad twin, whose name is
hell.

THAT'S MINE!

Ownership, that is the thing.
"That's mine" we all say.
And we say this of everything.
We are the possessors.
Individuals possessing everything
and all things.
"that's mine" should be marked
on every gravestone.
And with this noxious thought
comes pride.
If it is mine I am in charge,
I have authority.
What happens when your
authority is challenged?
A rise to defense and protection.
Thus, all challenge is a threat
that must be thwarted
by any means.
"That's mine!"
Back off, hands off, get away.
"That's mine!"
And thus, the battle is joined.
Could there be a better way?

Yes, there could and is
for certain.
It is found in humility.
Humility, the lubricant of peace.
Humility is the destroyer of pride.
Humility allows a man
to accept only what is his as
his possession.
Much of what is claimed "THAT'S MINE!,"
is really a gift.
Take life itself if you will.
Did you give it to yourself?
No, it is a gift to be nurtured
and cherished.
A gift to be honored in honor of the Giver.
The Giver, of course, is
God.

TALKING DONKEY

Have you ever heard a donkey
speak?
Human words that you could understand?
No, you haven't, but
Balaam did.
Way, way, way back when.
Balaam's donkey saw
Jesus as the Angel of the Lord.
Dressed in shining armor
and holding a
sharp sword in His hand.
The donkey saw Him but not his master, Balaam.
Then the donkey spoke,
the donkey spoke in human words
of warning.
These words from his donkey weren't enough
for Balaam.
He needed a bigger lesson.
Then Balaam could see this Majestic Jesus
in His Glory.
Then Balaam fell on his face
before Him,
Admitting he was a sinner.

And you?
Do you hear the donkey speak
and ignore as Balaam did?
Do you need a greater lesson too?
God's voice is always speaking,
do you ever hear?

FROM WHENCE WE COME

We humans started somewhere.
Started means beginning.
So, beginning it is.
Oh, yet so many variations.
Humans pondered from the start,
where did we start and when?
Have we always existed?
The evidence says not.
Now what?
Humans started somewhere,
at some time.
But what does time mean?
Has time itself always existed?
It's not easy to answer that one.
Oh, but wait, isn't time measured
by our galaxy, whatever that is?
Our home revolves around our sun,
and our home rotates too.
All so precise and nice and perfect.
Did we do that?
Did we spin our home to make time?
A difficult thought, indeed.
But is it?
The thought is really rubbish.

No humans made time exist.
It is folly to think we could.
Oh, pride and hubris
of the highest order are required
to believe this.
And also, how we started.
Did we humans create ourselves?
What we did do, however, is create
a fake.
Of course we didn't create ourselves.
But, just maybe, something else did.
We'll call it chance.
No, a better name is evolution.
That's it, evolution.
Millions and billions, let's make them trillions
of time units to fulfill.
And wo we nave the universe, and time,
and us.
So sweet and wonderful, a delusion

ABOUT THE AUTHOR

Mr. Lemon has an academic background.
He attended college and university, receiving an MFA
degree from the University of Chicago. Mr. Lemon also had
a college and university teaching career.
While attending Beloit College, Mr. Lemon studied under
Dr. Chad Walsh, poet-in-residence and prominent
American poet and writer. This experience occurred in the
early nineteen sixties, yet the impact stayed with him
through the years.
After a decades long career in the visual arts, Mr. Lemon
began writing essays that morphed into poems.

You will find as you read, Mr. Lemon writes from a

Christian World View. His hope is that Christians may be

encouraged, and others be moved in the direction of Jesus.

God bless all of you who read these poems.

ACKNOWLEDGEMENTS

The encouragement, patience, and loving support by my wife, Nancy, helped make this constant flow of poems have purpose. She never corrected but rather suggested, allowing me to adjust.

Brenda Spalding's guidance and effort and skill turned this book from dream to reality

My Christian faith, and thus, Jesus, provided most of the raw material. And, of course, the bible itself as the source of all Truth.

And Rev. Dr. Chad Walsh. A major name in American Poetry. Poet-in-residence at Beloit College and mentor from the grave. He was a sweet, kind man of great faith in Christ. As a friend of C.S. Lewis, he was one of the finest writers of the Twentieth Century, and he passed what he knew on to me.

www.ingramcontent.com/pod-product-compliance
Lightning Source LLC
Chambersburg PA
CBHW071524120626
46550CB00006B/2348

9 798988 740698